Praise for *Code Breaker*

"Brian Aspinall puts a very human face on coding and helps the reader understand it is not just for the computer geeks, but can be implemented for all grade levels in meaningful ways that help us see our world in a different way."

— George Couros,
author of *The Innovator's Mindset*

"Brian Aspinall passionately makes the case for coding and computational thinking in all classrooms using a variety of practical examples. It's not just about writing lines or placing blocks of code, it's about getting students to think about the curriculum in new and interesting ways using modern tools like Scratch and Minecraft. This book is for everyone who has ever asked, 'Why should I care about coding?' By the end of the story of the pooping baby, you will know why!"

— Matthew Oldridge,
speaker, writer, and mathematics educator

"This book is a must for anyone looking to thoughtfully integrate coding into curriculum beyond the #HourofCode. Brian not only provides a unique outlook on how we should view coding in the classroom, but shares tremendous insights into how to innovate the use of coding in learning beyond academic success or helping students be prepared to 'get a job.' With creative lessons masterfully woven throughout the book, this is a read that is set to inspire and guide anyone looking to infuse more creativity into classroom learning."

— Michael Cohen,
speaker, innovation consultant, and author of *Educated by Design*

"Brian Aspinall has created a valuable resource that not only will help educators deepen their understanding of computer coding, but one that makes the case for how all educators can use the concepts of computational thinking to shape their pedagogy and instructional practices to increase student learning."

— Laura Fleming,
library media specialist and author of *Worlds of Making*

"This book is a must-read for any teacher interested in learning more about the rationale for teaching coding in class and how to begin. With sample lesson plans and personal stories with his students, Brian Aspinall breaks down how to use coding principles in many subject areas, including math, geometry, algebra, science, and language arts. I particularly enjoyed the chapter where he interviewed other classroom teachers who are teaching coding with success with students as young as kindergarten! I have admired Brian for many years for his ability and determination to convince teachers about the importance of coding in any curriculum. It was a pleasure to read about his journey with teaching, who influenced him along the way, and what he believes today's classroom should look like."

— Sylvia Duckworth,
speaker, tech coach, and author of *Sketchnotes for Educators*

"When I think of coding in the classroom, one of the first names that comes to my mind is Brian Aspinall. This little book is a great tool to have at your disposal and to share with others! Tips, stories, and so much more make this book a must-buy!"

— Todd Nesloney,
award-winning educator and co-author of the book *Kids Deserve It*

"Teachers are eager to get started coding in the classroom and this is the perfect quick and easy guide! Aspinall walks us through the foundational theory of maker education and leads the reader through introductory coding lessons both with and without a computer."

— Colleen Graves,
co-author of *The Big Book of Makerspace Projects* and
20 Makey Makey Projects for the Evil Genius

"Brian Aspinall is an exemplary computer science teacher and valued member of the global computer science community. I have always viewed Brian as my go-to person when it comes to coding, and, more importantly, the pedagogy around coding. Brian's book, *Code Breaker*, provides an incredibly valuable context for anyone interested in teaching coding, already teaching coding, or for that matter, teaching in general. The book tackles the more important question of 'Why coding?' rather than simply serving as another book on how to code. I am admittedly not much of a reader but Aspinall's book is an easy and engaging read. The engaging part makes perfect sense as you delve into Brian's philosophy on teaching. In the book, Brian coins the term, 'classroom engagement' (compared to classroom management) and this notion of creating a truly engaging environment for students is at the heart of the book. Dig in and you will get a glimpse at where Aspinall developed an interest in teaching as well as his evolved approach to teaching and learning. The book provides the reader the feeling of being on the journey with Brian through his conversational tone and witty storytelling. I mean, the book starts with the story of how one student's fascination with poop led to his mastery of geometry and coding.

"I have been following Brian for some time and have grown quite fond of his work. I am glad to consider him a colleague, role model, and friend. Brian has always been accessible and willing to engage in discussions related to his (and my) passion. It is no surprise that his book provides a wonderful overview of his approach to teaching and his evolution as an amazing educator. The book is inspiring, just like the author. His passion comes right off of the pages, and as you read you feel yourself transforming as a teacher and a student. Brian's approach to the world of coding takes us away from the analytical, robotic thoughts many have about coding and into the human, logical side of why coding and problem solving are so important in education. Kudos to Brian for allowing his true self to come through his writing. A must-read whether you're interested in coding or just a great outlook on pedagogy and the notion of engaging students in the learning process."

— Steven Isaacs,
teacher, Minecraft mentor, and Minefaire producer

Code
BREAKER

Increase
Creativity
Remix
Assessment
and Develop
a Class of
Coder Ninjas!

Brian Aspinall

Code Breaker: Increase Creativity, Remix Assessment, and Develop a Class of Coder Ninjas!
© 2017 by Brian Aspinall

This book is available at special discounts when purchased in quantity for use as premiums, promotions, or fundraisers or for educational use. For inquiries and details, contact the publisher at books@daveburgessconsulting.com.

Published by Dave Burgess Consulting, Inc.
San Diego, CA
http://daveburgessconsulting.com

Cover Design by Genesis Kohler
Editing and Interior Design by My Writers' Connection

Library of Congress Control Number: 2017961273
Paperback ISBN: 978-1-946444-54-7
Ebook ISBN: 978-1-946444-55-4

First Printing: December 2017

*To Steph, for the GNR concerts, Songbird,
Woodstock, and life at the beach.
Keep on rockin' in the free world!*

Contents

o   o   o   o   o   o   o   o

Preface..xiii

Chapter 1: The Clarity of Poop.......................1

Chapter 2: A Wing and a Papert.......................7

Chapter 3: What It Looks Like to Me.................15

Chapter 4: A Peak Inside My Classroom..............25

Chapter 5: How Other Teachers Do It................43

Chapter 6: Grit, Perseverance, and Alzheimer's:
           Why Coding Matters......................55

TEDx Talks...59

Other Resources....................................61

References...63

More from Dave Burgess Consulting..................67

About the Author...................................79

*#ShoutOut to the wonderful Meagan Gillmore!
You have a unique gift for bringing people's ideas
to print. I am forever grateful.*

Preface

0　　　0　　　0　　　0　　　0　　　0　　　0　　　0

REMEMBER WHEN WE USED TO GO TO THE LIBRARY TO GET INFORMATION? In many ways, I suppose we still do. The point is, we live in an era of access. Answers to knowledge-based questions reside in databases and can be quickly retrieved with the touch of a button.

It wasn't always like this. Some of us remember the pre-Internet world. Many of us have forgotten. But even before the information age, as far back as the 1960s, educators used coding to teach kids by using kinesthetic activities. Reggio Emilia has inspired millions with play-based learning, and one of my personal heroes, Seymour Papert, taught geometry using a robotic turtle.

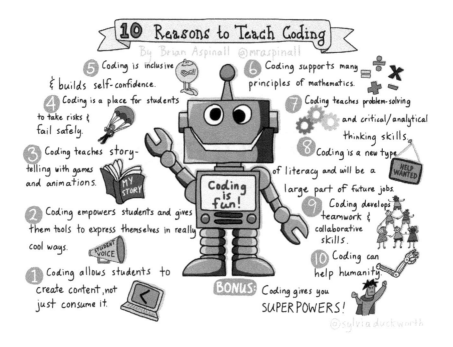

I'm what many define as a self-taught coder. I have fond memories of learning HTML and JavaScript in the early 1990s after watching my dad write web-based software.

Toward the end of that decade, Y2K nearly brought the house down. Fortunately for a large mining company in northern Ontario, my uncle thought critically and wrote software to save them from going back in time. Imagine a multi-million-dollar business operating on one's thoughts and ideas so that a ticking computer clock doesn't roll over to 1900. One man, one machine, one idea at the heart of the unearthing of a new century. Although he doesn't gloat about the experience, this massive organization ran smoothly on those corrected lines of codes. He didn't even ask for a promotion.

Chapter 1

THE CLARITY OF POOP

A POOPING BABY SHOWED ME HOW I WANTED TO TEACH.

It was my first year teaching a Grade 8 class, and it wasn't exactly my dream job. I loved learning basic HTML as a teenager in the 1990s, and I earned an undergraduate computer science degree at the University of Windsor in Ontario, Canada. When I finished teachers' college, also at Windsor, I hoped to teach math and computer science in high school, but like many new graduates, I latched onto whatever jobs were available in my area. It wasn't high school or math or computer science, but it was a job.

But I couldn't kick the computer coding bug. I'd decided to become a teacher partly because of my experiences as a counselor at a kids' summer technology camp. I wanted to share that same enthusiasm with students during the school year, so I started an after-school computer coding club. Students learned to code with Scratch, the program developed by MIT's Mitch Resnick. Today it seems everyone who's interested in teaching kids how to code uses Scratch, but this was the mid-2000s, years before initiatives such as Hour of Code. The software had to be installed on every computer, because it wasn't web-based as it is today. And I had as much to learn as the students did! I had worked with Java in college and taught HTML, but I had never linked blocks of code together as you do in Scratch. What I might have lacked in experience with the program, I made up for with enthusiasm. I threw myself into teaching students about loops and variables, and they quickly caught on.

Many of my colleagues were not as excited. They didn't blatantly discourage me from pursuing the club; they were just skeptical about using computer coding as a teaching tool.

Maybe I was a little skeptical too. My personality isn't suited for worksheets or rote learning. I did well in my computer science courses, in part because I never had to memorize syntax. Still, I knew standard teaching practices favor memorization and rote learning. I also knew it would take creativity to show some people the value of coding.

One of my students, Jaime, demonstrated this vital connection when he decided to code his first game. He called it "Pooping Baby." The game involved moving an infant across the screen as it shot poop missiles, but it was far more than a gag to generate laughs: It was an application of our geometry curriculum. For the baby to move to the left, the student had to change the X variables to be negative. Moving the baby up and down required changing the Y variables. Before the baby could shoot poop missiles, the proper X and Y coordinates had to be plotted. Within that game, the concepts I'd been teaching on paper came alive on the screen—albeit with poop!

FEATURED POST

HUBBUB! CODING A FIRST NATIONS' GAME OF CHANCE

http://brianaspinall.com/
hubbub-coding-a-aboriginal-game-of-chance

The best part was that Jaime was having so much fun, he probably didn't realize he was mastering geometry skills and meeting his school's curriculum expectations. But I did. I saw his work, and I saw the kind of teacher I wanted to be. I wanted students to see curriculum expectations as skills, and I wanted them to gain those skills in the same way this student made his game—by being creative, taking risks, making mistakes, and receiving feedback. The student who designed Pooping Baby saw patterns in the world and applied what he saw to create real solutions to real problems.

Watching Jaime code his first game reminded me of how my Grade 11 media studies teacher, Mrs. Boudreau, let me make a website for a presentation on a pop icon, when the assignment originally asked me to make a poster. Back then, I'd thought the biggest struggle would be convincing her that a site dedicated to Tupac Shakur was appropriate for school. I might never know exactly what she thought about my musical tastes, but I know her decision to let me explore my interests in a creative way set me on the path that led to this student's game. Because Mrs. Boudreau had said yes to me, I knew I couldn't say no to Jaime and his Pooping Baby game. Learning, like the game's content, is messy!

FEATURED POST

FLIPPING A COIN WITH PYTHON

http://brianaspinall.com/
coding-probability-simulators-with-python-csforall

This student was one of my greatest teachers. He inspired me to learn more about how computational thinking and coding can be used in the classroom and across subjects and how it can benefit students throughout their lives.

After watching that student succeed in a virtual context, I wanted to explore using the same process in the nonvirtual world. That's why I've written this book—not a small feat for a regular blogger who sometimes still struggles with spelling. What you are about to read are lessons I've learned as I've used computational thinking in my teaching. We'll get into some theory along the way, sure. While I was bringing coding to my classroom around 2006, Jeannette Wing and her team at Microsoft were introducing the world to the concept of computational thinking. The way she defines it, computational thinking is the synergy of the human mind and the power of machines. Her ideas, and the work of others, such as Mitch Resnick's teacher Seymour Papert, have influenced my own teaching practices. But before I learned those theories, I saw how they applied to the classroom. Those classroom experiences are what I want to share with you.

I hope this book helps you see how theories about computational thinking can apply to your classroom, whether you're a computer science geek like me or not. I want you to think about and reflect on your own teaching pedagogy and perhaps challenge it as well. *Code Breaker* isn't a how-to manual. You are you. I am me. I don't know your students. What's worked in my class might not work in yours, and that's OK. You probably have some things to teach me as well. The greatest teachers are those who keep learning. As a child, my Poppa was one of my favorite teachers. He showed me how to mix chemicals and how to change variables and watch for different outcomes. This experimental approach to discovery is in many ways like coding. Try, observe, try again, fail, try again, succeed. I wish math class were like that. Poppa was also a geologist, and he taught me how to inspect fool's gold and other minerals. His hands-on approach to learning continues to guide my practice of discovery and teaching to this day.

The stories you are about to read are based on information I have observed, perceived, and been given. Any mistakes are my own. Let's take this journey together.

FEATURED POST

10 REASONS KIDS SHOULD CODE

http://brianaspinall.com/
10-reasons-kids-should-learn-to-code

Chapter 2

0 0 0 0 0 0 1 0

A WING AND A PAPERT

HERE'S A SECRET: THIS BOOK DOESN'T BELONG TO ME.

Sure, my name is on it as the author and all of that. But none of what you're about to read is purely original. Like all teachers, I am a student. I have had the opportunity to learn about both computer science and teaching (Is it an art? A science? Both? Is this debate even helpful?). Before I share more about my personal approach to teaching—why I think we should teach students computational thinking, the role of technology in the classroom, and all that—I need to explain some of the theories that have shaped my understanding of education. Don't worry—I'll keep this short.

Featured Post

Coding Rock Paper Scissors

http://brianaspinall.com/
coding-rock-paper-scissors-to-teach-probability

A major shift in education theory has taken place in the past decade or so. Many learning spaces have gone from quiet rows to loud centers. We used to think that a well-managed classroom was a quiet classroom. Several people, including myself, are questioning this assumption. I do not think these attitudes, and the ways of teaching that result, help produce the kind of learners we want our students to be: risk takers, collaborators, and critical thinkers. In fact, I think these "traditional" (for lack of a better word) teaching methods actually work against creating this sort of learner.

I'm not alone in my beliefs about how education needs to change, and my thoughts aren't new, either. Theorists have been discussing these ideas for decades.

Consider Jean Piaget, one of the most influential child psychologists of the twentieth century and the father of "constructivism."

Many of us had to study his theories in our education courses, and for good reason! His theory attempts to describe how individuals, especially children, make meaning of the world based on the interactions between their experiences of the world and their ideas about the world. Others' theories of constructivism examine how an individual's interactions with society influence how they understand the world; this is commonly known as "social constructivism." Piaget was largely focused on the individual and genetic makeup. He wanted to know how individuals' interactions with themselves influenced how they understood reality. He was so fascinated by this question that he observed his own children to help develop his theories.

I value many things about Piaget's theories. He emphasized the role of play in education, for example. His ideas about how we respond to knowledge are also quite helpful. He talked about the difference between "assimilation" of knowledge and "accommodation" of knowledge. When we assimilate knowledge, we incorporate the new things we have learned into our current understanding of the world, but we don't change the framework through which we understand the world. Accommodation is different. We learn new things, but we change our framework of the world to adjust for this new information. Our view of the world constantly changes as a result of what we learn, allowing us to use failures as opportunities to learn and grow. This can help us take risks and think creatively because we know failure will not shatter our perception of the world. I try to encourage my students to think this way.

But I'm not as enthusiastic about some of the other ways Piaget's theories can be applied in the classroom. He spent a lot of time focusing on a child's individual development, even dividing it into separate stages. These stages might help parents and teachers better understand how children are progressing and identify where they are excelling and where they might need help. We see the influence of this belief that children complete certain tasks in stages in many areas of classroom design and teaching. For example, we group students by age. We have expectations of what they should complete at each age level before they move on to the next. In education, we are always preparing for what will happen next.

Although Piaget's theory has substance, I can't help but wonder whether these ideas of defined benchmarks set people up for a one-size-fits-all model. If we acknowledge kids as individuals, with their own strengths and weaknesses, constructivism doesn't appear to make sense beyond simple age-appropriate benchmarks.

But I am incredibly grateful to Piaget because his theories were influential to Seymour Papert, a man many consider to be the father of modern artificial intelligence. His book *Mindstorms*, published in 1980—the year Piaget died—is a treasure of thoughts about education and helping students love learning. Papert developed a theory called "constructionism," which asserts that people learn best about the world when they are involved in making— constructing—things in the world. To do this, children need to have some control over their own learning.

Papert championed the use of computers and computer technology to teach children. He especially saw the value of using these technologies to teach math. For him, math was not just a collection of concepts to be memorized. It was more of a place: somewhere children could explore and learn to love. He coined the term "Mathland"—a place where children see math in their everyday lives. Because children can see how math applies to everyday tasks—including, and perhaps especially, activities they enjoy—they naturally come to enjoy math. Math is something to explore. Mistakes become a learning tool. As children learn to self-correct, they develop new ways to solve problems and embrace uncertainty.

FEATURED POST

INDIGENOUS TRAIL TREES AND CODING A MICRO:BIT COMPASS

http://brianaspinall.com/
indigenous-trail-trees-coding-a-microbit-compass

Papert believed education should be concrete, that students should see how concepts in the classroom apply to their lives outside of the classroom. He thought computers were a good tool to teach this. He developed Logo Turtle, a program in which users create line graphics by entering commands. If this sounds similar to Scratch, a coding program that allows children to make characters by putting blocks of text together, don't be surprised. Papert worked at MIT—the same place where Mitch Resnick developed Scratch.

But Papert was saddened by the use of computer labs—restricting computers, and students' use of those computers, to a specific location. He believed that was simply applying old methods of teaching with new technology. He was, in many respects, ahead of his time. In later years, he expressed sadness that so many people were slow to adopt his ideas or seemed to misunderstand them. But some people did understand them.

One of those is Jeannette Wing, an MIT graduate and corporate vice president of research at Microsoft. In 2006, she introduced the term *computational thinking,* a synergy between the human mind and the power of machines. She noted that the widespread use of computers made it necessary for everyone to learn how to think in this way. This was similar, she said, to the way the printing press influenced education. That technology made it essential that everyone learn to read, write, and do basic math. "Computational thinking is a fundamental skill for everyone," she wrote.

FEATURED POST

WHAT IS COMPUTATIONAL THINKING?

http://brianaspinall.com/
what-is-computational-thinking

But Wing stressed that teaching computational thinking was not the same as teaching computer coding. Coding was an application of computational thinking. Humans might use computers to express their computational thinking, but, she said, computational thinking is not about how computers think—it's actually about how humans think.

Wing outlined many characteristics of computational thinking. It is about conceptualizing, so it is more than just coding or programming. She said it is a fundamental skill, not a rote one. By *fundamental,* she meant a skill that everyone must know to function well in society. *Rote* is a way to remember or express that skill. Wing wrote that computational thinking is at the heart of engineering and mathematics, but she emphasized that all people need to learn to think this way. The ideas, she said, are more important than the artifacts or tools—in this case, computers—that express them.

Wing wrote for an academic audience, but she wanted these ideas to grab hold outside of academia. She particularly wanted teachers to understand these concepts and pass them on to their students.

As a teacher, I was beginning to see the value of Wing's ideas before I learned about her writing or the work MIT had done to teach kids coding using Scratch. Her work described something I already knew to be real, something I was trying—and continue to try—to bring into my own teaching and classrooms.

Chapter 3

0 0 0 0 0 0 1 1

WHAT IT LOOKS LIKE TO ME

NOW THAT WE'VE COVERED OTHER PEOPLE'S TEACHING PHILOSOPHIES, I WANT TO INTRODUCE YOU TO MINE. Here's what I believe:

I believe we need to change the way we think about teaching. But that doesn't mean we need to download every app, participate in every #edchat, and post every class assignment to Instagram. Just because you've changed the technology you use in your classroom doesn't mean you've changed the way you think about your role in the classroom. In fact, the more I think about changing my classroom practice, the less I think about technology.

"But wait!" I can hear you protest. "Brian, didn't you study computer science? Isn't that what this book is about?" Yes, I studied computer science. Computer technology helped motivate me to become a teacher. I was programming before I was preparing lessons. Part of the reason I don't think about technology much when I think about changing my classroom perspective is this: I don't need to. Technology is such a regular part of my life, I don't consciously consider it. To borrow an old question: Do fish realize they're wet? I swim in technology.

But to answer your second question: This book is not simply about technology. This book is about changing how we think about *teaching*, and sometimes that means learning about and using new technologies.

Let me explain what I mean by discussing how we talk about coding. A lot of resources are out there to help teachers incorporate coding into their classes and teach students how to code. That's great—in fact, there are some at the end of this book! But before you skip to those pages, we need to consider why we're teaching kids to code.

We contradict ourselves a lot as teachers. We don't like "industrial education" these days. We'd rather group our classrooms into learning centers and clusters than have students sit in rows. We're also moving away from worksheets and rote memorization. After all, the logic goes, teaching is partly about preparing students for the real world, and that world includes jobs. Many of these industrial teaching strategies were created to help students get jobs in factories. Because work has changed, we need to change how we teach. We need to prepare students with new skills for new jobs.

We say we should teach students how to code. The Internet is connected to everything—literally, as the growing Internet of

Things shows. With coding skills, students can get good jobs and be competitive in the workforce. Do you see what we've done here? Essentially, nothing. We still think the end goal of teaching is simply helping kids get jobs. Our reason for teaching hasn't changed, just the materials we use to teach. We say we want students to direct their learning, to be creative individuals. And then we give them all the same device and tell them to download the same programs and tell ourselves that approach, in and of itself, makes us creative, innovative, progressive teachers. How different is this, really, from giving all of our students the same notebook and pencil?

FEATURED POST

UNPLUGGING THE HOUR OF CODE
PART 1

http://brianaspinall.com/
unplugging-the-hour-of-code

One of the reasons we've convinced ourselves that introducing these technologies automatically makes us creative is that we're thinking about coding in the wrong way. We tend to think coding is the same as computer science. It's not. (Remember the degree I have? Trust me, not all my courses were about coding.) Computer science is about how things work and how we can make them work better. Coding and hardware are ways to do that. Coding is a part of computer science, just as biology is one area of study in the natural sciences. We would never say science is only biology, so why do we act like computer science is only coding?

The key to computer science—and as a result, coding—is thinking. People express their thoughts in language. So it might help to think about coding as a language. Although we have language classes, we use languages in all subjects. We teach kids to read so they can learn from others, not so they can become professional readers. We teach kids to write so they can communicate, even though we know only a few will get jobs as writers.

FEATURED POST

CODING A STORY:
PROBABILITY AND QUICK WRITE PROMPTS

http://brianaspinall.com/
coding-a-story-probability-quick-write-prompts

We need to think about teaching kids to code in the same way. Sure, the Internet of Things means more jobs will require coding. But most students are not going to become professional programmers—just as most students do not become professional writers. That's OK. They still should learn to code. They still should learn a different way of thinking, communicating their thoughts to others, and learning what others think.

If we want to help children think differently, and maybe better, we need to encourage them to have growth mindsets. That means we need to encourage them to adapt to change, take risks, and learn from their mistakes without thinking they're failures because they made a mistake. They must to learn to communicate and collaborate. They must to learn to face their fears and not get stuck in them. We should also remind ourselves that even students who get good grades can get stuck in a mindset of fear that resists growth.

Let's look at two students:

Student A loves school and is good at "playing school." She participates in class discussions and thrives on the challenge of a test. School comes naturally to Student A, but she also works at it. In fact, she studies at least three nights ahead of every exam and completes her homework as soon as she gets home from school.

Why? Because Student A is driven by grades, and she wants to be told what to do to hit the mark. For her, earning a good grade equals success. Student A knows what to do to get the grade, and Student A feels successful.

Student A doesn't take risks or think critically, because she has already figured out exactly what is required to earn high marks. Veering from that path is unsafe and puts her high marks at risk. Staying on that path is the safe choice.

Student B doesn't like school and is disengaged. In fact, if Student B could only get a B on his report card, it would be a rare cause for celebration. There could be many reasons for this. Maybe Student B was never taught how to take a test properly, so the test-based system tells Student B that he is dumb. This just makes it easier for Student B to check out of school. He doesn't complete homework, but that doesn't mean he doesn't think about it. In fact, Student B's fear of failing—and feeling like failure is his only option—often keeps him awake at night. Why? Because Student B is also driven by marks, but he doesn't know how to excel to earn those good marks. For Student B, getting a good mark also equals success, but he doesn't know how to do well on tests and exams. He doesn't think critically because he figures Student A has all the answers, and if she already knows the answer, his opinion won't matter. Student B won't take a risk. It's unsafe.

These two students bring home vastly different report cards, but they have one thing in common—fear of trying new things and growing.

We all know several factors contribute to a student becoming Student A or Student B—family life, native language, learning disabilities, physical disabilities, class size, school culture, and administration, to name a few. And let's be brutally honest: one of the hard truths about teaching is that we see the impact of all of these things but cannot always do much about their causes. We can't go home with our students, but we can control our classrooms. We can encourage our students to grow. I suggest we begin by changing how we think about control and classroom management.

A classroom isn't made up of walls and ceilings and desks and curriculum. Classrooms are made up of people. We are asked to manage people.

People make noise. People make mistakes. We need to stop thinking a *controlled* classroom is a quiet classroom, and an *uncontrolled* classroom is a loud one. The volume in a classroom is not a scale to measure the quality of the teacher in it. A loud classroom doesn't equal a bad teacher; a quiet classroom doesn't equal a good teacher.

As teachers, we all want students to meet our expectations. We want them to do well and push themselves to do better. I also want them to want to do better. I want reluctant writers to write, not avoid it because they're afraid of messing up or disappointing me. I want them to write because they know I already believe in their ability. They want to make me happy, but not because they're afraid of making me mad. They know that what they write or don't write won't change my belief in what they can do as students. They're engaged students.

FEATURED POST

CODING AN INTERACTIVE MAP OF CANADA

http://brianaspinall.com/
coding-an-interactive-map-of-canada

Maybe we need to change the phrase *classroom management* to *classroom engagement*. Our goal as teachers should be to help students become engaged with learning. This comes through collaboration and discussion—making noise. Sometimes it means watching students work and asking them questions about what they're doing. It means letting them show us what they're doing, and not just us telling them what to do.

Student engagement can be hard to measure, especially with the way most assessments are done. I'm not the biggest fan of worksheets and rote memorization—they don't work with my personality—but I understand they have their place. I just don't think they should be the only form of assessment or measure of accomplishment.

FEATURED POST

CODING FRACTAL ART WITH PYTHON

http://brianaspinall.com/
creating-fractal-art-using-python-ctmindset

For example, we often use a student's ability to remember facts quickly as a way to measure knowledge. In this view, the better students are students who can recall information quickly. A good math student, in this view, isn't just one who has memorized all his multiplication tables. A good student is someone who can spout all the correct answers really, really fast. Speed is what sets them apart.

For too long, we've made time the constant in schools. We expect students to all work on the same timeline. We placed kids in isolated settings, started a countdown, and judged them based on their performance in that moment, and quite often, only that moment. If students don't give us the results we want in the time we want, we say they've failed.

I admit, I don't like assigning letter grades to students. I'd remove them from elementary grades, if possible. I think assessments and evaluations with rigid frameworks and closed-ended questions make it hard to incorporate open-ended computational thinking activities into classroom management and teaching practices. We say all students can achieve. We say we want them to take risks. But too often, our assessment practices don't reflect those beliefs.

We tell students about how great inventors tried and failed many times before they succeeded, but we don't always take risks in our teaching. Maybe we need to reconsider our fixation with time. Maybe we should teach students to create content without the burden of time constraints. This could help create environments in which they know they're free to fail, and it would allow educators to focus more on the process of learning and not only on the final product. It might take a long time to reach the destination, but the blood, sweat, and tears put into the project would be more than worth it.

We must find a balance between simply asking students to regurgitate content and helping them create content. Somewhere in that middle ground, we must provide opportunities for students to generate their own solutions.

We need to stop trying to make kids conform to our world and, instead, embrace theirs.

FEATURED POST

MAKEY MAKEY WHACK A MOLE!

http://brianaspinall.com/
makey-makey-whack-a-mole

Chapter 4

0   0   0   0   0   1   0   0

A PEAK INSIDE MY CLASSROOM

I'VE USED CODING ACTIVITIES AND THE CONCEPTS OF COMPUTATIONAL THINKING TO TEACH A VARIETY OF SUBJECTS. We use the logic of computational thinking a lot; we just don't realize that is what we're doing.

I've written some stories about how computational thinking has found its way into my lessons. I want to say this happened because of my own knowledge and skill, but more often than not, students are the ones who've encouraged me to try this. Warning: These are not polished lesson plans. I'm not a perfect teacher, and these stories reflect that. But I hope they give you some ideas about how you can bring these concepts to your class, and how your students might encourage you to take these ideas even further.

Math

Computer science is about learning different languages. This first activity shows how to use computer science to teach literacy and numeracy. Remember, coding is only a snippet of computer science. I like computer science because it helps students practice computational thinking. Computational thinking is about breaking down problems and thinking in algorithms, logical reasoning, debugging, analyzing, simulating, and problem solving, all of which can be done without technology.

Exponents, Number Patterns, and Coding

- Big Ideas: Exponents, Patterns, Base 10, Base 2, Order of Operations
- Task: Explain to students that a binary string of eight bits is a byte.
- eg, 10111011—Each digit is a bit; eight bits is a byte (four bits is a nibble)
- Computers understand machine language (1s and 0s) and must convert it into "human" language.
- Show students an example of an ASCII table.

Dec	Hex	Oct	HTML	Chr	Dec	Hex	Oct	HTML	Chr
0	0	000		NULL	64	40	100	&#064;	@
1	1	001		Start of Header	65	41	101	&#065;	A
2	2	002		Start of Text	66	42	102	&#066;	B
3	3	003		End of Text	67	43	103	&#067;	C
4	4	004		End of Transmission	68	44	104	&#068;	D
5	5	005		Enquiry	69	45	105	&#069;	E
6	6	006		Acknowledgment	70	46	106	&#070;	F
7	7	007		Bell	71	47	107	&#071;	G
8	8	010		Backspace	72	48	110	&#072;	H
9	9	011		Horizontal Tab	73	49	111	&#073;	I
10	A	012		Line Feed	74	4A	112	&#074;	J
11	B	013		Vertical Tab	75	4B	113	&#075;	K
12	C	014		Form Feed	76	4C	114	&#076;	L
13	D	015		Carriage Return	77	4D	115	&#077;	M
14	E	016		Shift Out	78	4E	116	&#078;	N
15	F	017		Shift In	79	4F	117	&#079;	O
16	10	020		Data Link Escape	80	50	120	&#080;	P
17	11	021		Device Control 1	81	51	121	&#081;	Q
18	12	022		Device Control 2	82	52	122	&#082;	R
19	13	023		Device Control 3	83	53	123	&#083;	S
20	14	024		Device Control 4	84	54	124	&#084;	T
21	15	025		Negative Ack.	85	55	125	&#085;	U
22	16	026		Synchronous Idle	86	56	126	&#086;	V
23	17	027		End of Trans. Block	87	57	127	&#087;	W
24	18	030		Cancel	88	58	130	&#088;	X
25	19	031		End of Medium	89	59	131	&#089;	Y
26	1A	032		Substitute	90	5A	132	&#090;	Z
27	1B	033		Escape	91	5B	133	&#091;	[
28	1C	034		File Separator	92	5C	134	&#092;	\
29	1D	035		Group Separator	93	5D	135	&#093;	]
30	1E	036		Record Separator	94	5E	136	&#094;	^
31	1F	037		Unit Separator	95	5F	137	&#095;	_
32	20	040	&#032;	Space	96	60	140	&#096;	`
33	21	041	&#033;	!	97	61	141	&#097;	a
34	22	042	&#034;	"	98	62	142	&#098;	b
35	23	043	&#035;	#	99	63	143	&#099;	c
36	24	044	&#036;	$	100	64	144	&#100;	d
37	25	045	&#037;	%	101	65	145	&#101;	e
38	26	046	&#038;	&	102	66	146	&#102;	f
39	27	047	&#039;	'	103	67	147	&#103;	g
40	28	050	&#040;	(	104	68	150	&#104;	h
41	29	051	&#041;	)	105	69	151	&#105;	i
42	2A	052	&#042;	*	106	6A	152	&#106;	j
43	2B	053	&#043;	+	107	6B	153	&#107;	k
44	2C	054	&#044;	,	108	6C	154	&#108;	l
45	2D	055	&#045;	-	109	6D	155	&#109;	m
46	2E	056	&#046;	.	110	6E	156	&#110;	n
47	2F	057	&#047;	/	111	6F	157	&#111;	o
48	30	060	&#048;	0	112	70	160	&#112;	p
49	31	061	&#049;	1	113	71	161	&#113;	q
50	32	062	&#050;	2	114	72	162	&#114;	r
51	33	063	&#051;	3	115	73	163	&#115;	s
52	34	064	&#052;	4	116	74	164	&#116;	t
53	35	065	&#053;	5	117	75	165	&#117;	u
54	36	066	&#054;	6	118	76	166	&#118;	v
55	37	067	&#055;	7	119	77	167	&#119;	w
56	38	070	&#056;	8	120	78	170	&#120;	x
57	39	071	&#057;	9	121	79	171	&#121;	y
58	3A	072	&#058;	:	122	7A	172	&#122;	z
59	3B	073	&#059;	;	123	7B	173	&#123;	{
60	3C	074	&#060;	<	124	7C	174	&#124;		
61	3D	075	&#061;	=	125	7D	175	&#125;	}
62	3E	076	&#062;	>	126	7E	176	&#126;	~
63	3F	077	&#063;	?	127	7F	177	&#127;	Del

ASCII Table
http://www.asciichars.com

- Provide students with this "code" sheet or one you have created and have them "chunk" the bits into strings of eight, one byte, in the boxes underneath.

What does this say?

0101001001100001011011100110010001101111011011101

Their job is to follow the instructions—your lesson—and convert each eight-digit byte into a decimal value. They will look up the decimal value in the ASCII chart and find the corresponding alphabet letter. We are solving for a six-letter word (*Random*). Yes, it is case-sensitive.

Once you have the fundamental understanding of how to convert binary to decimal, you can create some pretty unique learning opportunities. You could create scavenger hunts by hiding binary code around the school or behind QR codes. Maybe you want to support narrative writing by incorporating binary "code" into stories for readers to crack.

Learning about exponents can be tricky. This method might offer some opportunities to scaffold and differentiate learning. You might wish to provide different students with different binary code. What I love most about activities like this is how the math is the skill needed to complete something more, something bigger. Simply solving a math problem isn't the point. The math leads to something else.

Using Scratch to Teach Math

Math textbooks often teach concepts in strands and topics that are isolated from each other. Coding tools such as Scratch help a math curriculum become "spiral," allowing it to show how different areas of math are connected.

Scratch is ideal for this. Developed based on principles of geometry, it allows students to translate *sprites* (the graphical characters they create within the program) across a screen, store information in variables, and use number sense to make calculations.

Here are some ways I've used Scratch and other coding activities to teach different math lessons:

Factors

When I started teaching math, I would often assign students worksheets with a large number of questions. That's what I was taught to do. But I started to notice some patterns, and you've probably seen this in your classrooms. Some students grasp the concepts right away and finish all of their work. Others never finish all the questions.

I saw this happen often when teaching students how to find the factors of a composite number. I often gave students questions that started with phrases such as, "List the factors of (certain number)," or "What are the factors of (certain number)?" These questions were asking students the same thing.

After reflection, I decided I would rather have them tell me the process for finding the factors of a number. After all, if students could explain how to find the factors of one number, they could find the factors of any given number.

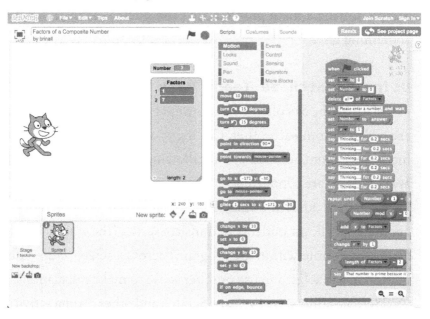

Here's the tricky thing: We can easily look up how to find the factors of a number online. Once we had written the procedure as a class, I challenged them to plunk each line into Scratch to see whether we could build an app that can find factors

This task provides many entry points for students, letting them work at their own levels. Differentiated learning is built into its design. Some students made an app with only the minimum requirements, but others expanded their scope. One student duplicated her code because she wanted her app to find the greatest common factor of two numbers. Her app even told me that 11 is a prime number because it has only two factors. She then used her app to solve the questions I'd been giving students from the textbook.

As an aside, having students write out a problem-solving process or procedure can also work well in a language arts class.

Geometry

Our experience with the factors app motivated me to incorporate computational thinking into my geometry units. These activities work especially well with lessons about location and movement.

You could create a pseudo code as a class. It might look something like this:

Move (NUMBER)	Move (NUMBER_UNTS)	TRANSLATE (NUMBER_UNTS)
Turn (LEFT / RIGHT)	Turn (+ -)(NUMBER)	ROTATE (+ -)(NUMBER)
Hop	Hop (Height)	Hop (Height_UNITS)
k-3	4-6	7+

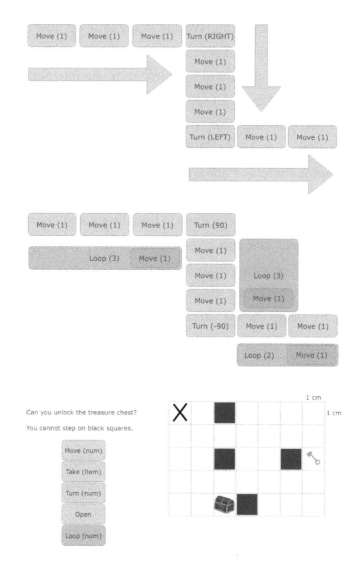

After you've made the block code language the whole class will use, you can create unique tasks using principles of geometry. You can challenge students to "code" each other. Pair them up and assign one student to be the robot and one the coder. It is the coder's job to navigate the robot (FriendBot) around an obstacle course in the classroom or hallway. Challenge them to code their FriendBots to deliver a message to the principal.

Alternatives to this task might include having students create games using grid paper. Allow students opportunities to create something at their level to challenge their friends.

Ultimately, the goal is to view location and movement as an algorithm.

Probability

I always find it hard to teach experimental and theoretical probability.

Early in my career, I would distribute coins and ask kids to make a T-chart. We would flip the coin once and record results. We'd flip it twice and record results. We'd then flip it three times and record results. Nobody would have fifty-fifty as a result because we had only flipped three times. I would then ask students to flip the coins a dozen or so times and record their results.

My goal was always to get them to construct their own knowledge of probability through this process. In reality, the lesson turned the classroom into a noisy jungle with change flying across the room. Students pretended to care but were not engaged in the activity. It wasn't until a student presented the idea of coding a coin-flipping simulator that my mindset changed. I assigned him the task and told him he would be a superstar if he could pull it off.

For the next few days, he spent most of math class working on what today we would call his "passion project." His parents reported that he also worked on it at home. But I didn't realize how engaged he'd become in the project until he and his friends showed up at school to present the final project before classes had started for the day. He assured me the simulator worked, and I asked him what he would like to do with it.

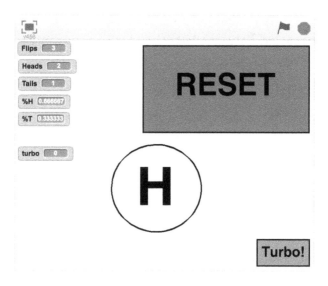

"Let's flip the coin a million times," he said with an evil tone.

"Yes, yes," I replied with an equally dark tone. "Let's do that."

I dedicated the SMARTBoard computer to his simulator, and we began to watch it run. What is most significant about this story is just how engaged these boys had become with a math assignment. They tried to sneak a peek whenever they could. They stayed in at recess and even stayed after school. Unfortunately, his coin flipper only made it to roughly 700,000 flips by the end of the day. But the results were fifty-fifty to about the ninth decimal place. I looked at them in astonishment and began to explain the Law of Large Numbers.

My explanation wasn't needed.

"Yeah, yeah, we get it," they said, and off home they went.

Algebra and Minecraft

We often teach growing patterns in algebra by standing in front of a class and projecting images onto the screen. We use the images to help discuss equations.

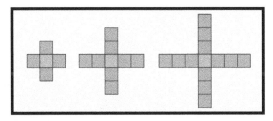

In the traditional sense, I wanted students to use words to explain how this pattern was growing. Figure 1 has five tiles. Figure 2 has nine. Figure 3 has thirteen. Using these data, we can create an algebraic equation to determine how many tiles will be in each figure.

Term #	Term Value
1	5
2	9
3	13

Pattern Rule: 4n + 1

Here's the problem: My old-school pedagogy attempted to force students to see this growing pattern as I did. In fact, if they didn't create this table of values, I would have marked their work incorrect.

I didn't change my thinking until a student suggested that each figure was actually a pyramid and not flat. You could hear the brain matter shift as my mind was blown. The student then suggested he build this growing pattern as he saw it, using Minecraft. Immediately, I felt ashamed. The pattern could be extended in an infinite number of ways. If students saw it differently than I did, that was OK. I felt as though I had let previous students down by not allowing them to show me this concept through a different lens.

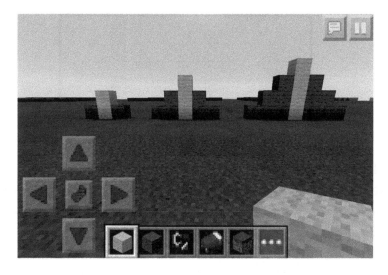

This concept also helped me teach spatial sense in a much deeper way. I asked the student whether the middle cube was still a constant in the pyramid, as it was in the flat image. I should have known what was coming.

I immediately raced home, hoping to change my plans for the following day. I soon realized that all learners should have the opportunity to design, build, and extend growing patterns as they see fit—as long as they can generate a table of values and an algebraic equation. We spent the next week or so designing Minecraft games in which kids built castles that contained different growing patterns. Players had to solve the growing pattern and find the appropriate sign before heading to the next room. The mazelike scenarios allowed all students to learn because they were naturally designed for scaffolding and differentiated learning.

Science

The real teachers in this story are my Grade 8 students. As a science teacher, I've always loved teaching the particle theory. Granted, I haven't always approached the topic in the most exciting way. I used to make students memorize the criteria. I'm sure some of you can say them with me:

- Particles have spaces between them.
- Particles are attracted to each other.
- Particles are always moving.
- Particles speed up and spread apart when heated.

It's pretty routine stuff. But one day, I witnessed a student have the biggest "Aha!" moment I've ever seen. As we looked over the textbook, I mentioned the squiggly lines and suggested that meant movement. I will never forget what happened next.

"You mean those particles are moving?" yelled a boy from the back.

Yet again, I was ashamed. I had been butchering the particle theory for years by assuming kids knew that squiggly lines in a textbook meant the particles were moving. Nope. Once again, I was reminded that kids often see the world differently.

I asked him to code the particle theory instead of memorize a list of bullet points. I wanted him to learn the list as a result of the coding process.

After all, if he could simulate moving particles that speed up and spread apart with heat, we were golden.

I mentioned before how Scratch uses principles of geometry to work, how it can help connect various strands within one subject. It's also great for showing how completely different subjects relate to one another.

Consider this student's simulator. The student moved particles (science) by plotting them on a Cartesian grid using random coordinates (geometry).

Talk about cross-curricular teaching!

Language Arts

Conditional statements, also known as Boolean logic, are fundamental components to computer science. They're also a big part of how we write procedures. Here is a great way to teach conditional statements in primary health class. This example shows how to use conditional statements to write the procedure for brushing teeth.

"Traditional" Procedure for Brushing Teeth

- Get your toothbrush.
- Get the toothpaste and apply a small dab to the brush.
- Turn your toothbrush to a 45-degree angle and brush back and forth, beginning with your molars.
- Repeat the third step for all other teeth.
- Turn on tap.
- Fill a cup with water.
- Turn off tap.
- Drink water. Swish water around in your mouth.
- Spit out toothpaste.
- Clean sink.

Take this procedure and break it into modules. Each module is a small procedure on its own, and you can scaffold groups of kids accordingly to provide necessary differentiated instruction. The goal here is to write the algorithm for brushing teeth as a class. Each group provides a module of instruction. Each module depends on other modules to make this work.

To further challenge students and teach them about equity, ask an additional question: "What if we don't have toothpaste?"

(Quite a few things need to be in place before someone can write a procedure about how to brush her teeth. One is, of course, toothpaste.)

```
If (HaveToothpaste) -> BrushTeeth()
//BrushTeeth is a module
Else (GetToothpaste)
//GetToothpaste is a module
```

This example requires two different modules or procedures. Expanding on them would look something like this:

```
GetToothpaste(
if(HaveNeighbors) ->GoToNeighborsHouse()
//Another module or procedure
else(
    if(HaveVehicle) -> DriveToStore()
//Another module or procedure
))
```

Some modules are easier to write than others. It can be difficult to think in algorithms at first, but it becomes more natural the more you do it. For example, the popular board game Monopoly is full of algorithms.

```
if(PassGo) -> Collect $200
if(InJail)
    if(RollDoubles) -> GetOutOfJail
    else(StayInJail)
```

The Code for Coding

If you've missed me saying this before, let me repeat myself: Computer science is not only coding, and coding should not be limited to computer class.

I recognize that computer class is a separate class in some schools and that some of you might only want my advice on teaching coding. So here are some of my thoughts on how to teach code. I've created a continuum with four phases: BOSC.

B: Bot coding

Under Bot coding, teachers and students learn about block code. They run through games and tutorials to move objects from one point to another to complete a task. Levels are scripted, and there is no open space, just a linked set of block code instructions to move a bot. Bot coding is a great place to model math concepts such as estimating distance and moving across a grid.

O: Open-space coding

In this category, coders are familiar with block code and understand how to link it. Using tools such as ScratchJr, Hopscotch, and Scratch, coders use block code to create games, stories, and simulations. Possibilities are endless, but coding modules are limited to the functions within the app itself.

S: Syntax coding

Like open-space coding, users start with a blank slate and begin to think critically, solve problems, and code applications using syntax. Coders at this level are learning language. They're making the language of coding work on their own. This gives them many more opportunities to be creative.

C: Collaborative coding

Coders at this level have a firm understanding of syntax, computational thinking, and logical reasoning. They use existing frameworks and APIs (Application Program Interfaces) to make improvements to existing applications. These coders also make use of open sources and build applications. They are, simply, coder ninjas.

Chapter 5

HOW OTHER TEACHERS DO IT

I'VE TALKED A LOT ABOUT COLLABORATION IN THIS BOOK AND HOW IT IS IMPORTANT FOR STUDENTS AND TEACHERS TO LEARN FROM EACH OTHER. With that in mind, I have included a few stories from other teachers about how they are incorporating these concepts into their classes. I've learned a great deal from these educators, and I hope you do as well.

Grade 1 Coding Experts

Jessica Konecny (@MrsKonecny) teaches Grade 1 in Chatham, Ontario, Canada. She is always willing to try new things. When she started exploring coding with her students, I immediately became interested. I teach Grade 8, so I wanted to know what it's like teaching coding in the primary grades. Here's what Jessica told me in an email interview:

What made you decide to try coding with your Grade 1 class?

Our school has talked a lot about the benefits of coding, and we had Grade 8 students do a workshop to teach us how to use Minecraft. I decided to give coding a try due to Twitter. There was a week dedicated to #HourOfCode.

FEATURED POST

UNPLUGGING THE HOUR OF CODE PART 2

http://brianaspinall.com/
unplugging-the-hour-of-code-part-2

What have you noticed as a result?

Students are very engaged in the process of coding. They are more willing to make mistakes and debug problems rather than give up. Some of my students that struggle with math have been able to demonstrate a strong sense of spatial awareness, which is generally a difficult topic. Experts have arisen that the students naturally go to for help.

You had students code in the physical space using linking cubes. Can you tell me about that?

While searching #HourOfCode on Twitter, I saw pictures of another Grade 1 teacher, @avivaloca, using the app Lightbot. I downloaded it onto my tablet and for that week I put it under the HoverCam, and we solved levels as a class. We started by having one student try at a time, and then we used white dry-erase boards for the whole class to code individually before they checked their work. It was a great week! The students loved the app, and many put it on their own devices at home. While it was successful, I didn't know how to apply it to the curriculum at that time, so we stopped after a week.

We recently started a geometry unit in math that included 2D and 3D shapes, as well as spatial awareness with direction. We also started a structure unit in Science and discussed how to make a stable structure. That's when Lightbot came back in full force! Groups used pictures from each level to make the structures out of snap cubes. Then they wrote the code onto sticky notes. Eventually students built the Lightbot structures, wrote the code, and checked their work individually. Now we are finishing making our own stable structures and coding directions to light up specific cubes in two different ways. Students demonstrate their knowledge at their level, and we cover both math and science.

Where do you see your students taking this?

With Lightbot, we plan to show other classes in the school our work. We have also been Tweeting out our progress, which has resulted in new connections and great feedback. Our goal is to have a coding night for our parents to come see our work.

Our next goal is to use ScratchJr to animate our narratives and enhance our Social Studies ideas.

Finally, is there any other information you'd like us to know about this project and approach to learning?

I didn't know anything about coding before I tried this. I used trial and error, which was great for my class to experience. Oftentimes, they were teaching me a faster or easier way to work the program.

We did this all with one tablet, even though I have access to a class set. I think it's important to code and use technology because it serves a purpose and not just for the sake of saying you did it.

When I opened the structure and coding assignment, the students surpassed my expectations. They included several lights, jumps, and turns. Their creativity really shined.

We are always looking to make connections and find new ways to show our learning!

Jessica's story taught me about teaching elements of computer science without using a computer. I learned about how to use math manipulatives to do "physical" hacking. Her students ran algorithms in the "real world" before testing them out on

Lightbot. Her story also demonstrates how these skills can apply to several subjects.

This example shows the importance of teamwork and learning through trial and error. Jessica got interested in bringing this to her students after another class conducted a workshop on coding. She knew she wasn't an expert, but she succeeded by being willing to rely on her students for help.

FEATURED POST

LEARN TO CODE SPACE SHOOTER

http://brianaspinall.com/
space-shooter

Giving Students a Voice

Valerie Volland (@MrsVolland1) is a colleague of mine who teaches Grade 5. She uses Hopscotch as a coding tool—and for demonstrating learning with her students. Val had never coded before she started doing this, so I asked her for a reflection.

What made you decide to try coding with your Grade 5 class?

I decided to try coding with my class after one of our P.A. Day Ed Camp–style meetings. At this meeting we had students from our school teach us about coding, and we discussed the idea of Hour of Code. I had no idea what coding really was, so I thought I'd better invest some time and learn. We started with Hopscotch because you are able to use it on a tablet, and it is age appropriate.

What have you noticed as a result?

The first day we tried Hopscotch, I gave the students the opportunity to explore and problem solve on their own or with a partner. The second time we used Hopscotch, some students were already becoming "experts." I noticed that the students would share their learning and collaborate and try to problem solve together. Many students put the app on their own devices, and they watched YouTube videos at home and at school to help them create new codes.

You had students code applications to draw 3D math shapes. Can you tell me about this?

We started out by creating 2D shapes. We had great discussions about the importance of knowing the angle degrees and the number of sides when creating the code. We also noticed a pattern that happens when creating some of the shapes, and that you can reduce the amount of coding by creating loops. After mastering the 2D shapes, I challenged them to try to create 3D shapes. They amazed me, of course. They worked together to problem solve and persevere through this challenge. The mathematical discussions and collaboration were incredible. Some students even thought to bring out a protractor to help with the angles. We noticed that there were different ways to create 3D shapes, different codes and strategies. I love when they realize that there is more than one way to solve a problem!

Where do you see your students taking this?

I think the next step will be to try to find other classes through Twitter that use Hopscotch, so we can share and challenge each other. I was also thinking that we could try to use Hopscotch to make translations. I would also like to get them to use Scratch as a next step, where they can learn to make apps. They seem to be picking up the concepts so fast. It is very exciting.

Finally, is there any other information you'd like us to know about this project and approach to learning?

I think one of the most important things that I have learned from this experience is that using technology with math helps to even out the academic playing field. I have 10 students that have IEPs (Individual Education Plans) in my classroom, and with the use of this technology, you are not able to pick out who needs accommodations in math. This coding experience also gives voices to students who previously, for one reason or another, did not share their thoughts or opinions. It has empowered them. This adventure has been a great learning experience for my students and myself. I enjoyed being a student right along with them. For anyone who is thinking about trying coding with their students, my advice would be, "Don't think; just do!" Let go of wanting to be in control and embrace the opportunity to be a co-learner.

Val's story demonstrates how anyone, at any age, can learn coding. It also brings up something we talk about a lot when we talk about twenty-first-century learning—equity and student voice. Equity means that everyone gets what they need—not that everyone necessarily gets the same thing. That can be a difficult concept for students to understand; they often know if they're different. Val had students who needed different supports in math to learn the content. Individualized Education Plans can be useful, but the system can sometimes make it hard for all students to feel included. Coding allowed all students to participate together. It helped give everyone a tool to speak and let their voices be heard.

FEATURED POST

CODING NON-LINEAR STORIES WITH TWINE

http://brianaspinall.com/
coding-non-linear-stories-with-twinethreads

Five-Year-Olds Coding Without Technology

I haven't just learned about teaching from my own colleagues. I have also had the privilege to hear from educators around the world.

In the previous chapter, I talked about how you can use coding concepts to teach your students about location by having them "code" each other. Here's an example of how a teacher applied a similar concept to teaching young students about language.

Melissa Dann (@meld70) is a prep teacher in Melbourne, Australia, who has begun exploring the concepts of coding with her five-year-old students. She sent me an email reflecting on her practice. I've copied it in full below, with her permission:

Hi Brian,

Here is a quick overview of what's been happening in my classroom teaching coding to five-year-olds. (Just a reminder that we have been at school for twelve weeks—it's amazing!)

Game: Robots and Programmers

Children work in pairs. One child is the Robot. The other is the Programmer.

Language development is an important part of the activity. Programmers can ask Robots to take steps, turn, jump, hop, etc. Programmers cannot ask their Robots to do anything dangerous. Programmers must say "please" or the Robot will not respond. This is similar to the game Simon Says, where the children don't respond unless the command is prefaced with "Simon says," and saying "please" is just good manners.

I kept it to a maximum of 10 steps as the children were keen to ask their robot to take 100 or even 1,000 steps. We realized—by counting how many steps it took to cross the room—that 10 was about the right amount for the size of our room. Also, I place a big emphasis on counting accurately. Some of these children cannot count accurately to 20 yet, and if they can, some don't have 1-to-1 correspondence to 20. For the children who are very capable, they can ask their robot to move 5 plus 5 steps, or 2 less than 8 steps, double 2 steps, etc. The children have to be able to work the answer out before the Robot can move.

> Programmer: Take 10 steps.
>
> Robot: You didn't say 'Robot, please.'
>
> Programmer: Robot, please take 10 steps.
>
> Robot: 1,2 … 10 (counting steps).
>
> Programmer: Robot, please turn a quarter.
>
> Robot: Which way?
>
> Programmer: (Using spinner, turns spinner) That way, right. (pointing right)
>
> Programmer: Robot, please turn a whole circle.
>
> Programmer: Robot, please take 4 steps backwards.
>
> Robot: 1, 2, 3, 4
>
> Programmer: Robot, please take 5 plus 3 steps.
>
> Robot: How many is that? (Programmer and Robot count on their fingers, 5 plus 3.)

After playing this game the first time, it became apparent that we needed a way to decide how far a turn was, eg, ¼ turn, ½ turn. So we made spinners with ¼ turn, ½ turn, and full turn and that showed left and right. This is still a difficult concept, but I am persevering. We also started using Bee-Bot on Friday, and the spinners were helpful as each press of the turn button on the Bee-Bot is a quarter turn.

We have also played outside on the playground, and this led to a lot more use of location language.

It has been interesting to watch the dynamics between the pairs of children. As with all activities, some groups were very focused, others not so. One group was very silly until the children swapped roles, and then they were much more focused. I asked them at the end whether it was easier being a Robot or a Programmer. One child, who was the Programmer first, had found it very hard to be the Programmer and think of things to ask their partner to do; hence the lack of focus. But when they swapped roles, they had enjoyed being a Robot.

It's been a great learning experience for me, and I have been thinking about blogging it—haven't done a professional blog before.

Thanks for your encouragement and support.

Cheers!

Melissa's story is a great example of a teacher using what students use in their lives outside of the classroom to teach lessons inside the classroom. As a bonus, it can literally get students outside of the classroom—a change I think even we teachers appreciate! This activity demonstrates how computer coding is a language while also building children's language skills and honing their ability to work well together. I think it could also be adapted to help teach other languages such as French or Spanish. This would also make it suitable for older children.

Chapter 6

GRIT, PERSEVERANCE, AND ALZHEIMER'S: WHY CODING MATTERS

AT THE BEGINNING OF THIS BOOK, I SAID A POOPING BABY SHOWED ME THE KIND OF TEACHER I WANT TO BE.

Sometimes, though, being the teacher who encourages students to think critically and creatively, and who willingly learns and makes mistakes alongside them, makes me want to curl up like a baby and have someone else do the hard work for me. It's exhausting.

When I need encouragement to continue being a teacher who pushes beyond rote memorization and routine assessments, when I need motivation to encourage students to take risks, think critically, and solve problems in the middle of challenging situations, I turn to Street View in Google Maps and type in a familiar address. I click on the slider and watch images pass until it stops on a shot taken in 2009.

I usually try not to cry as a picture of one of the greatest teachers I've ever had comes on the screen.

The man in the picture looks out onto the street as if he were expecting to pose for the camera, but I am sure he never expected his image to be captured and archived online. In fact, I'm not even sure if he would have been able to describe the truck that drove by that day or tell you the number on the old brick farmhouse behind him—98.

But when I see that elderly man in a blue baseball cap, jeans, and a sweater, I see a giant of perseverance. That man is my late Poppa, as my brother and I called him. For much of my childhood and adolescence, my brother and I would spend our March school breaks with our grandparents in Toronto. We'd board the train in Windsor, and our grandparents would pick us up at Toronto's Union Station. Poppa was a retired geologist and high school science teacher. He would show us rocks and minerals, and we would mix chemicals together. Chemical reactions happened right before our eyes. Some would call it a makerspace, or at the very least, an extra assignment that reinforced what we were learning in science class. For us, it was simply spending time with Poppa.

Poppa was diagnosed with Alzheimer's a few years before that Street View photo was taken. The diagnosis devastated me.

I knew he'd lose his ability to communicate. Our science lessons would change.

As it turned out, he would continue to teach me. I watched him, trying to understand the disease wreaking havoc on his mind. It was as if I were at a zoo, studying Alzheimer's.

FEATURED POST

LEARN TO CODE TENNIS FOR ONE

http://brianaspinall.com/
tennis-for-one

One day I saw him try to remove the storm windows from the storm porch at the front of the house. I emphasize "try"—he'd done this with little effort for more than thirty years. This time was different. Because of the disease, he couldn't remember the right tools to use. He struggled with finding the proper screws. He didn't have the right screwdriver or bit, and his mind couldn't tell him which ones he needed.

I watched him struggle with the task for fifteen minutes. I also saw him persevere to solve the problem. As he fumbled with screwdrivers and screws, he was holding fast to his mental grit even as Alzheimer's ravished his brain.

His life was an example of all the theories we talk about in textbooks and the philosophies I want to bring to my teaching: observing problems in the world around us and persevering to find solutions to them.

Regardless of whether he meant to, he was teaching me to never give up, the same lesson I hope my students learn through coding.

When Poppa first removed the storm windows on his home, he never would have imagined a picture of him standing in front of those windows would be stored online, or that I would still find comfort in it years after his death. But thanks to a few coders, it is, and I do. The world has changed radically; we communicate and interact with each other in such vastly different ways now. We change technology, and technology changes us.

The need to persevere through life's difficulties has not changed. It is not going to change. The biggest challenges and problems in life that our students will face won't be solved by an app. But the way they learn to think while they use emerging technologies can help them find solutions.

My Poppa reminds me why I love technology and why I want students to create with technology. It's not because of the way it has helped me teach lessons or solve household problems. It's because it's given me richer ways to interact with people. Nothing changes how we think more than the ways we interact with others.

TEDx Talks

0   1   0   1   0   1   0   0

brianaspinall.com/tedx-talks

Beyond Rote Learning (Chatham, ON)
Published March 14, 2014

Education Reform (Chatham, ON)
Published June 16, 2015

Hacking the Classroom (Kitchener, ON)
Published June 16, 2016

Other Resources

0   1   0   0   1   1   1   1

MINECRAFT LESSONS:

- http://www.hourofcuriosity.com/minecraft

AUGMENTED REALITY LESSONS:

- http://www.hourofcuriosity.com/submit-an-activity-2

CODING VIDEO TUTORIALS:

- http://www.hourofcuriosity.com/coding

GETTING STARTED WITH MAKEY MAKEY:

- http://www.hourofcuriosity.com/makey-makey

GETTING STARTED WITH MICRO:BIT:

- http://www.hourofcuriosity.com/microbit

References

0   1   0   1   0   0   1   0

Berry, Miles. *Computing in the National Curriculum. A Guide for Primary Teachers*. Bedford, UK: Computing at School, 2013.

Bers, Marina Umaschi, Louise Flannery, Elizabeth R. Kazakoff, and Amanda Sullivan. 2014. "Computational thinking and tinkering: Exploration of an early childhood robotics curriculum." *Computers & Education*, 72: 145–57. doi:10.1016/j.compedu.2013.10.020.

Drake, Susan. 2014. "Designing across the curriculum for "sustainable well-Being": A 21st century approach." *Essay in Sustainable well-Being: Concepts, issues, and educational practice*, edited by Frank Deer, Thomas Falkenberg, Barbara McMillan, and Laura Sims, 57–76. Winnipeg, MB: Education for Sustainable Well-Being (ESWB) Press. www.eswb-press.org/uploads/1/2/8/9/12899389/sustainable_well-being_2014.pdf#page=65.

Fullan, M. (2013). *Great to excellent: Launching the next stage of Ontario's education agenda*. Toronto: Ontario Ministry of Education. Retrieved from: http://www.michaelfullan.ca/wp-content/uploads/2013/09/13_Fullan_Great-to-Excellent.pdf.

Gadanidis, George. 2012. "Why can't I be a mathematician?" *For the Learning of Mathematics*, 32 (2): 20–26. http://researchideas.ca/documents/05-Gadanidis.pdf.

Gadanidis, George. 2015. "Coding as a Trojan Horse for Mathematics Education Reform." *Journal of Computers in Mathematics and Science Teaching*, 34(2): 155-73.

Gadanidis, George. 2015. *Coding for Young Mathematicians*. London, Ontario, Canada: Western University.

Gao, Xin, and Jennifer Grisham-Brown. 2011. "The Use of Authentic Assessment to Report Accountability Data on Young Children's Language, Literacy and Pre-Math Competency." *International Education Studies*, 4 (2). doi:10.5539/ies.v4n2p41.

Graf, Edith Aurora, and Meirav Arieli-Attali. 2015. "Designing and Developing Assessments of Complex Thinking in Mathematics for the Middle Grades." *Theory Into Practice*, 54 (3): 195–202. doi:10.1080/00405841.2015.1044365.

Hargreaves, Eleanore. 1997. "Mathematics Assessment for Children with English as an Additional Language." *Assessment in Education: Principles, Policy & Practice*, 4 (3): 401–12. doi:10.1080/0969594970040306.

Harlen, Wynne, and Jan Winter. 2004. "The development of assessment for learning: learning from the case of science and mathematics." *Language Testing*, 21 (3): 390–408. doi:10.1191/0265532204lt289oa.

Jeltova, Ida, Damian Birney, Nancy Fredine, Linda Jarvin, Robert J. Sternberg, and Elena L. Grigorenko. 2011. "Making Instruction and Assessment Responsive to Diverse Students' Progress: Group-Administered Dynamic Assessment in Teaching Mathematics." *Journal of Learning Disabilities*, 44 (4): 381–95. doi:10.1177/0022219411407868.

Kafai, Yasmin B., and Quinn Burke. "Computer Programming Goes Back to School." *Phi Delta Kappan*, 95, no. 1 (2013): 63-65.

Kazakoff, Elizabeth R., and Marina Umaschi Bers. "Put Your Robot in, Put Your Robot out: Sequencing through Programming Robots in Early Childhood." *Journal of Educational Computing Research*, 50, no. 4 (2014): 553-73. doi:10.2190/ec.50.4.f.

Kazakoff, Elizabeth R., Amanda Sullivan, and Marina U. Bers. "The Effect of a Classroom-Based Intensive Robotics and Programming Workshop on Sequencing Ability in Early Childhood." *Early Childhood Education Journal*, 41, no. 4 (2012): 245-55. doi:10.1007/s10643-012-0554-5.

Levine, Rachel. *Curriculum-based dynamic assessment emphasizing a triarchic model and language abilities: examining the utility of this testing method in elementary school mathematics classrooms.* PhD diss., 2009. (Order No. 3349141). Available from ProQuest Education Journals. (305047877). Retrieved from http://search.proquest.com/docview/305047877?accountid=15115.

Liang, Xin. "Assessment use, self-efficacy and mathematics achievement: comparative analysis of PISA 2003 data of Finland, Canada and the USA." *Evaluation & Research in Education*, 23, no. 3 (2010): 213-29. Retrieved from http://search.proquest.com/docview/868061586?accountid=15115.

Morten Misfeldt, Stine Ejsing-Duun. "Learning mathematics through programming: An instrumental approach to potentials and pitfalls." Konrad Krainer; Nada Vondrová. CERME 9-Ninth Congress of the European Society for Research in Mathematics Education, Feb 2015, Prague, Czech Republic. pp.2524-2530, Proceedings of the Ninth Congress of the European Society for Research in Mathematics Education.

Morgan, Candia, Anna Tsatsaroni, and Stephen Lerman. 2002. "Mathematics Teachers Positions and Practices in Discourses of Assessment." *British Journal of Sociology of Education*, 23 (3): 445–61. Retrieved from http://search.proquest.com/docview/206172116?accountid=15115.

Nguyen, Diem M, Yi-Chuan Hsieh, and Donald G Allen. 2006. "The Impact of Web-Based Assessment and Practice on Students' Mathematics Learning Attitudes." *Journal of Computers in Mathematics and Science Teaching*, 25 (3): 251–79. Retrieved from http://search.proquest.com/docview/220630959?accountid=15115.

"21st Century Competencies: Foundation Document for Discussion." 2016. Ontario Ministry of Education. http://www.edugains.ca/resources21CL/About21stCentury/21CL_21stCenturyCompetencies.pdf.

"The Ontario Curriculum Grades 1-8: Mathematics." 2005. Ontario Ministry of Education. http://www.edu.gov.on.ca/eng/curriculum/elementary/math18curr.pdf.

Papert, Seymour. 1993. "Turtle geometry: A mathematics made for learning." *Mindstorms: Children, Computers, And Powerful Ideas*. New York: Basicbooks.

Resnick, Mitchel, John Maloney, Andrés Monroy-Hernández, Natalie Rusk, Evelyn Eastmond, Karen Brennan, Amon Millner, et al. 2009. "'Digital Fluency' Should mean designing, creating, and remixing, not just browsing, chatting, and interacting." *Communications of the ACM*, 52 (11): 60–67.

Sammons, Kay, et al. 1992. "Linking instruction and assessment in the mathematics classroom." *The Arithmetic Teacher*, 39 (6): 11. Retrieved from http://search.proquest.com/docview/208771651?accountid=15115.

Smith, Carmen Petrick, and Maureen D. Neumann. 2014. "Scratch it out! Enhancing Geometrical Understanding." *Teaching Children Mathematics*, 21 (3): 185–88.

Sneider, Cary, Chris Stephenson, Bruce Schafer, and Larry Flick. 2014. "Teachers Toolkit: Exploring the Science Framework and NGSS: Computational Thinking in the Science Classroom." *Science Scope*, 038 (03): 10–15.

Suurtamm, Christine, and Martha J. Koch. 2014. "Navigating dilemmas in transforming assessment practices: experiences of mathematics teachers in Ontario, Canada." *Educational Assessment, Evaluation and Accountability*, 26 (3): 263–87. doi:10.1007/s11092-014-9195-0.

Suurtamm, Christine, Martha Koch, and Ann Arden. 2010. "Teachers' assessment practices in mathematics: classrooms in the context of reform." *Assessment in Education: Principles, Policy & Practice*, 17 (4): 399–417. Retrieved from http://search.proquest.com/docview/821956768?accountid=15115.

Thomas, Cathy Newman, Delinda Van Garderen, Amy Scheuermann, and Eun Ju Lee. 2015. "Applying a Universal Design for Learning Framework to Mediate the Language Demands of Mathematics." *Reading & Writing Quarterly*, 31 (3): 207–34. Retrieved from http://search.proquest.com/docview/1683616180?accountid=15115.

Wallace, Matthew. 2011. "Developing assessment practices: a study of the experiences of preservice mathematics teachers as learners and the evolution of their assessment practices as educators." Dissertation. (Order No. 3499583). Available from ProQuest Education Journals. (944324214). Retrieved from http://search.proquest.com/docview/944324214?accountid=15115.

Watson, Anne. 2006. "Some difficulties in informal assessment in mathematics." *Assessment in Education: Principles, Policy & Practice*, 13 (3): 289–303. Retrieved from http://search.proquest.com/docview/204048130?accountid=15115.

Wing, Jeannette. 2006. "Computational Thinking." *Communications of the ACM*, 49 (3): 33–35. http://www.cs.cmu.edu/afs/cs/usr/wing/www/publications/Wing06.pdf.

Yin, Yue, Judith Olson, Melfried Olson, Hannah Solvin, and Paul R. Brandon. 2015. "Comparing Two Versions of Professional Development for Teachers Using Formative Assessment in Networked Mathematics Classrooms." *Journal of Research on Technology in Education*, 47 (1): 41–70. Retrieved from http://search.proquest.com/docview/1646385125?accountid=15115.

More From

DAVE BURGESS
Consulting, inc.

Teach Like a PIRATE

Increase Student Engagement, Boost Your Creativity, and Transform Your Life as an Educator

By Dave Burgess (@BurgessDave)

Teach Like a PIRATE is the *New York Times'* best-selling book that has sparked a worldwide educational revolution. It is part inspirational manifesto that ignites passion for the profession, and part practical road map filled with dynamic strategies to dramatically increase student engagement. Translated into multiple languages, its message resonates with educators who want to design outrageously creative lessons and transform school into a life-changing experience for students.

Learn Like a PIRATE

Empower Your Students to Collaborate, Lead, and Succeed

By Paul Solarz (@PaulSolarz)

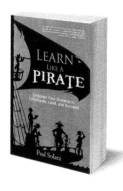

Today's job market demands that students be prepared to take responsibility for their lives and careers. We do them a disservice if we teach them how to earn passing grades without equipping them to take charge of their education. In *Learn Like a PIRATE*, Paul Solarz explains how to design classroom experiences that encourage students to take risks and explore their passions in a stimulating, motivating, and supportive environment where improvement, rather than grades, is the focus. Discover how student-led classrooms help students thrive and develop into self-directed, confident citizens who are capable of making smart, responsible decisions, all on their own.

P is for PIRATE

Inspirational ABC's for Educators

By Dave and Shelley Burgess (@Burgess_Shelley)

Teaching is an adventure that stretches the imagination and calls for creativity every day! In *P is for Pirate*, husband and wife team, Dave and Shelley Burgess, encourage and inspire educators to make their classrooms fun and exciting places to learn. Tapping into years of personal experience and drawing on the insights of more than seventy educators, the authors offer a wealth of ideas for making learning and teaching more fulfilling than ever before.

Play Like a Pirate

Engage Students with Toys, Games, and Comics

by Quinn Rollins (@jedikermit)

Yes! School can be simultaneously fun and educational. In *Play Like a Pirate*, Quinn Rollins offers practical, engaging strategies and resources that make it easy to integrate fun into your curriculum. Regardless of the grade level you teach, you'll find inspiration and ideas that will help you engage your students in unforgettable ways.

eXPlore Like a Pirate

*Gamification and Game-Inspired Course Design
to Engage, Enrich, and Elevate Your Learners*

By Michael Matera (@MrMatera)

Are you ready to transform your classroom into an experiential world that flourishes on collaboration and creativity? Then set sail with classroom game designer and educator Michael Matera as he reveals the possibilities and power of game-based learning. In *eXPlore Like a Pirate,* Matera serves as your experienced guide to help you apply the most motivational techniques of gameplay to your classroom. You'll learn gamification strategies that will work with and enhance (rather than replace) your current curriculum and discover how these engaging methods can be applied to any grade level or subject.

Pure Genius

*Building a Culture of Innovation and
Taking 20% Time to the Next Level*

By Don Wettrick (@DonWettrick)

For far too long, schools have been bastions of boredom, killers of creativity, and way too comfortable with compliance and conformity. In *Pure Genius*, Don Wettrick explains how collaboration—with experts, students, and other educators—can help you create interesting, and even life-changing, opportunities for learning. Wettrick's book inspires and equips educators with a systematic blueprint for teaching innovation in any school.

The Zen Teacher

*Creating Focus, Simplicity, and
Tranquility in the Classroom*

By Dan Tricarico (@thezenteacher)

Teachers have incredible power to influence—even improve—the future. In *The Zen Teacher,* educator, blogger, and speaker Dan Tricarico provides practical, easy-to-use techniques to help teachers be their best—unrushed and fully focused—so they can maximize their performance and improve their quality of life. In this introductory guide, Dan Tricarico explains what it means to develop a Zen practice—something that has nothing to do with religion and everything to do with your ability to thrive in the classroom.

140 Twitter Tips for Educators

Get Connected, Grow Your Professional Learning Network, and Reinvigorate Your Career

By Brad Currie, Billy Krakower, and Scott Rocco (@bradmcurrie, @wkrakower, @ScottRRocco)

Whatever questions you have about education or about how you can be even better at your job, you'll find ideas, resources, and a vibrant network of professionals ready to help you on Twitter. In *140 Twitter Tips for Educators*, #Satchat hosts and founders of Evolving Educators, Brad Currie, Billy Krakower, and Scott Rocco offer step-by-step instructions to help you master the basics of Twitter, build an online following, and become a Twitter rock star.

The Innovator's Mindset

Empower Learning, Unleash Talent, and Lead a Culture of Creativity

By George Couros (@gcouros)

The traditional system of education requires students to hold their questions and compliantly stick to the scheduled curriculum. But our job as educators is to provide new and better opportunities for our students. It's time to recognize that compliance doesn't foster innovation, encourage critical thinking, or inspire creativity—and those are the skills our students need to succeed. In *The Innovator's Mindset*, George Couros encourages teachers and administrators to empower their learners to wonder, to explore—and to become forward-thinking leaders.

50 Things You Can Do with Google Classroom

By Alice Keeler and Libbi Miller (@alicekeeler, @MillerLibbi)

It can be challenging to add new technology to the classroom but it's a must if students are going to be well-equipped for the future. Alice Keeler and Libbi Miller shorten the learning curve by providing a thorough overview of the Google Classroom App. Part of Google Apps for Education (GAfE), Google Classroom was specifically designed to help teachers save time by streamlining the process of going digital. Complete with screenshots, *50 Things You Can Do with Google Classroom* provides ideas and step-by-step instructions to help teachers implement this powerful tool.

50 Things to Go Further with Google Classroom

A Student-Centered Approach
By Alice Keeler and Libbi Miller
(@alicekeeler, @MillerLibbi)

Today's technology empowers educators to move away from the traditional classroom where teachers lead and students work independently—each doing the same thing. In 50 Things to Go Further with Google Classroom: A Student-Centered Approach, authors and educators Alice Keeler and Libbi Miller offer inspiration and resources to help you create a digitally rich, engaging, student-centered environment. They show you how to tap into the power of individualized learning that is possible with Google Classroom.

Master the Media

*How Teaching Media Literacy Can
Save Our Plugged-in World*

By Julie Smith (@julnilsmith)

Written to help teachers and parents educate the next generation, *Master the Media* explains the history, purpose, and messages behind the media. The point isn't to get kids to unplug; it's to help them make informed choices, understand the difference between truth and lies, and discern perception from reality. Critical thinking leads to smarter decisions—and it's why media literacy can save the world.

The Writing on the Classroom Wall

*How Posting Your Most Passionate Beliefs about
Education Can Empower Your Students, Propel Your
Growth, and Lead to a Lifetime of Learning*

By Steve Wyborney (@SteveWyborney)

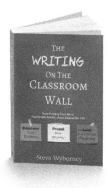

In *The Writing on the Classroom Wall*, Steve Wyborney explains how posting and discussing Big Ideas can lead to deeper learning. You'll learn why sharing your ideas will sharpen and refine them. You'll also be encouraged to know that the Big Ideas you share don't have to be profound to make a profound impact on learning. In fact, Steve explains, it's okay if some of your ideas fall *off* the wall. What matters most is sharing them.

Kids Deserve It!

Pushing Boundaries and Challenging Conventional Thinking

By Todd Nesloney and Adam Welcome
(@TechNinjaTodd, @awelcome)

In *Kids Deserve It!*, Todd and Adam encourage you to think big and make learning fun and meaningful for students. Their high-tech, high-touch, and highly engaging practices will inspire you to take risks, shake up the status quo, and be a champion for your students. While you're at it, you just might rediscover why you became an educator in the first place.

The Classroom Chef

Sharpen your lessons. Season your classes. Make math meaningful.

By John Stevens and Matt Vaudrey
(@Jstevens009, @MrVaudrey)

In *The Classroom Chef*, math teachers and instructional coaches John Stevens and Matt Vaudrey share their secret recipes, ingredients, and tips for serving up lessons that engage students and help them "get" math. You can use these ideas and methods as-is, or better yet, tweak them and create your own enticing educational meals. The message the authors share is that, with imagination and preparation, every teacher can be a Classroom Chef.

Ditch That Textbook

Free Your Teaching and Revolutionize Your Classroom

By Matt Miller (@jmattmiller)

Textbooks are symbols of centuries-old education. They're often outdated as soon as they hit students' desks. Acting "by the textbook" implies compliance and a lack of creativity. It's time to ditch those textbooks—and those textbook assumptions about learning! In *Ditch That Textbook*, teacher and blogger Matt Miller encourages educators to throw out meaningless, pedestrian teaching and learning practices. He empowers them to evolve and improve on old, standard, teaching methods. *Ditch That Textbook* is a support system, toolbox, and manifesto to help educators free their teaching and revolutionize their classrooms.

Your School Rocks ... So Tell People!

Passionately Pitch and Promote the Positives Happening on Your Campus

By Ryan McLane and Eric Lowe
(@McLane_Ryan, @EricLowe21)

Great things are happening in your school every day. The problem is, no one beyond your school walls knows about them. School principals Ryan McLane and Eric Lowe want to help you get the word out! In *Your School Rocks ... So Tell People!* McLane and Lowe offer more than seventy immediately actionable tips along with easy-to-follow instructions and links to video tutorials. This practical guide will equip you to create an effective and manageable communication strategy using social media tools. Learn how to keep your students' families and community connected, informed, and excited about what's going on in your school.

How Much Water Do We Have?

5 Success Principles for Conquering Any Change and Thriving in Times of Change

By Pete Nunweiler with Kris Nunweiler

In *How Much Water Do We Have?* Pete Nunweiler identifies five key elements—information, planning, motivation, support, and leadership—that are necessary for the success of any goal, life transition, or challenge. Referring to these elements as the 5 Waters of Success, Pete explains that like the water we drink, you need them to thrive in today's rapidly paced world. If you're feeling stressed out, overwhelmed, or uncertain at work or at home, pause and look for the signs of dehydration. Learn how to find, acquire, and use the 5 Waters of Success—so you can share them with your team and family members.

Instant Relevance

Using Today's Experiences in Tomorrow's Lessons

By Denis Sheeran (@MathDenisNJ)

Every day, students in schools around the world ask the question, "When am I ever going to use this in real life?" In *Instant Relevance*, author and keynote speaker Denis Sheeran equips you to create engaging lessons from experiences and events that matter to your students. Learn how to help your students see meaningful connections between the real word and what they learn in the classroom—because that's when learning sticks.

Launch

Using Design Thinking to Boost Creativity and Bring Out the Maker in Every Student

By John Spencer and A.J. Juliani
(@spencerideas, @ajjuliani)

Something happens in students when they define themselves as *makers* and *inventors* and *creators*. They discover powerful skills—problem-solving, critical thinking, and imagination—that will help them shape the world's future … *our* future. In *LAUNCH*, John Spencer and A.J. Juliani provide a process that can be incorporated into every class at every grade level … even if you don't consider yourself a "creative teacher." And if you dare to innovate and view creativity as an essential skill, you will empower your students to change the world—starting right now.

Teaching Math with Google Apps

50 G Suite Activities, Vol. 1

By Alice Keeler and Diana Herrington
(@alicekeeler, @mathdiana)

Google Apps give teachers the opportunity to interact with students in a more meaningful way than ever before, while G Suite empowers students to be creative, critical thinkers who collaborate as they explore and learn. In Teaching Math with Google Apps, educators Alice Keeler and Diana Herrington demonstrate fifty different ways to bring math classes into to the twenty-first century with easy-to-use technology.

Escaping the School Leader's Dunk Tank

How to Prevail When Others Want to See You Drown

By Rebecca Coda and Rick Jetter
(@RebeccaCoda, @RickJetter)

No school leader is immune to the effects of discrimination, bad politics, revenge, or ego-driven coworkers. These kinds of dunk-tank situations can make an educator's life miserable. By sharing real-life stories and insightful research, the authors (who are dunk-tank survivors themselves) equip school leaders with the practical knowledge and emotional tools necessary to survive and, better yet, avoid getting "dunked."

Start. Right. Now.

Teach and Lead for Excellence

By Todd Whitaker, Jeff Zoul, and Jimmy Casas
(@ToddWhitaker, @Jeff_Zoul, @casas_jimmy)

In their work leading up to Start. Right. Now. Todd Whitaker, Jeff Zoul, and Jimmy Casas studied educators from across the nation and discovered four key behaviors of excellence: Excellent leaders and teachers *Know the Way, Show the Way, Go the Way, and Grow Each Day*. If you are ready to take the first step toward excellence, this motivating book will put you on the right path.

Lead Like a PIRATE

Make School Amazing for Your Students and Staff

By Shelley Burgess and Beth Houf
(@Burgess_Shelley, @BethHouf)

In *Lead Like a PIRATE*, education leaders Shelley Burgess and Beth Houf map out the character traits necessary to captain a school or district. You'll learn where to find the treasure that's already in your classrooms and schools—and how to bring out the very best in your educators. This book will equip and encourage you to be relentless in your quest to make school amazing for your students, staff, parents, and communities.

Table Talk Math

A Practical Guide for Bringing Math into Everyday Conversations

By John Stevens (@Jstevens009)

Making math part of families' everyday conversations is a powerful way to help children and teens learn to love math. In *Table Talk Math*, John Stevens offers parents (and teachers!) ideas for initiating authentic, math-based conversations that will get kids notice and be curious about all the numbers, patterns, and equations in the world around them.

Shift This!

How to Implement Gradual Change for Massive Impact in Your Classroom

By Joy Kirr (@JoyKirr)

Establishing a student-led culture that isn't focused on grades and homework but on individual responsibility and personalized learning may seem like a daunting task—especially if you think you have to do it all at once. But significant change is possible, sustainable, and even easy when it happens little by little. In *Shift This!* educator and speaker Joy Kirr explains how to make gradual shifts—in your thinking, teaching, and approach to classroom design—that will have a massive impact in your classroom. Make the first shift today!

Unmapped Potential

An Educator's Guide to Lasting Change

By Julie Hasson and Missy Lennard (@PPrincipals)

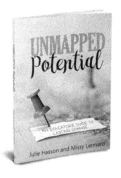

No matter where you are in your educational career, chances are you have, at times, felt overwhelmed and overworked. Maybe you feel that way right now. If so, you aren't alone. But the more important news is that things can get better! You simply need the right map to guide you from frustrated to fulfilled. *Unmapped Potential* offers advice and practical strategies to help you find your unique path to becoming the kind of educator—the kind of person—you want to be.

Shattering the Perfect Teacher Myth

6 Truths That Will Help You THRIVE as an Educator

By Aaron Hogan (@aaron_hogan)

The idyllic myth of the perfect teacher perpetuates unrealistic expectations that erode self-confidence and set teachers up for failure. Author and educator Aaron Hogan is on a mission to shatter the myth of the perfect teacher by equipping educators with strategies that help them shift out of survival mode and THRIVE.

Social LEADia

Moving Students from Digital Citizenship to Digital Leadership

By Jennifer Casa-Todd (@JCasaTodd)

Equipping students for their future begins by helping them become digital leaders now. In our networked society, students need to learn how to leverage social media to connect to people, passions, and opportunities to grow and make a difference. *Social LEADia* offers insight and engaging stories to help you shift the focus at school and at home from digital citizenship to *digital leadership.*

Spark Learning

3 Keys to Embracing the Power of Student Curiosity

By Ramsey Musallam (@ramusallam)

Inspired by his popular TED Talk "3 Rules to Spark Learning," this book combines brain science research, proven teaching methods, and Ramsey's personal story to empower you to improve your students' learning experiences by inspiring inquiry and harnessing its benefits. If you want to engage students in more interesting and effective learning, this is the book for you.

Ditch That Homework

Practical Strategies to Help Make Homework Obsolete

By Matt Miller and Alice Keeler
(@jmattmiller, @alicekeeler)

In *Ditch That Homework*, Matt Miller and Alice Keeler discuss the pros and cons of homework, why teachers assign it, and what life could look like without it. As they evaluate the research and share parent and teacher insights, the authors offer a convincing case for ditching homework and replacing it with more effective and personalized learning methods.

The Four O'Clock Faculty

A Rogue Guide to Revolutionizing Professional Development

By Rich Czyz (@RACzyz)

Author Rich Czyz is on a mission to revolutionize professional learning for all educators. In *The Four O'Clock Faculty*, Rich identifies ways to make PD meaningful, efficient, and, above all, personally relevant. This book is a practical guide that reveals why some PD is so awful and what you can do to change the model for the betterment of you and your colleagues.

Culturize

Every Student. Every Day. Whatever It Takes.

By Jimmy Casas (@casas_jimmy)

In *Culturize*, author and education leader Jimmy Casas shares insights into what it takes to cultivate a community of learners who embody the innately human traits our world desperately needs, such as kindness, honesty, and compassion. His stories reveal how these "soft skills" can be honed while meeting and exceeding academic standards of twenty-first-century learning.

About the Author

0   1   0   0   0   0   0   1

BRIAN ASPINALL is an educator, three-time TEDx speaker, coder, and consultant. Having worked with ministries, unions, universities, district and school teams, and corporations, he is an internationally recognized thought leader in digital skills education.

As a recipient of a Prime Minister's Award for Teaching Excellence in coding and computational thinking, Brian empowers educators to achieve more in the classroom using modern teaching tools and technology.

His enthusiasm, leadership, and approach to building capacity within STEM education has made him a sought-after speaker throughout North America and has earned him the honor of being selected as one of Canada's first Minecraft, Micro:BiT, and Makey Makey ambassadors!

Brian has been developing apps since the early 1990s, when his high school principal paid him to develop the school's first website. Unfortunately, neither the website nor the high school still exists.

To find out more about Brian Aspinall and his body of work, visit:

http://www.MrAspinall.com

http://www.BrianAspinall.com

Or, just Tweet him: @mraspinall

CPSIA information can be obtained
at www.ICGtesting.com
Printed in the USA
LVHW010021091118
596150LV00003B/124